D1518774

The Sillies

Written by Charnan Simon • Illustrated by Kathleen Petelinsek

Published in the United States of America by The Child's World®
PO Box 326 • Chanhassen, MN 55317-0326
800-599-READ • www.childsworld.com

Reading Adviser

Cecilia Minden-Cupp, PhD, Former Language and Literacy Program Director, Harvard Graduate
School of Education, Cambridge, Massachusetts

Acknowledgments

The Child's World®: Mary Berendes, Publishing Director

Editorial Directions, Inc.: E. Russell Primm, Editorial Director and Project Manager; Katie Marsico,
Associate Editor; Judith Shiffer, Assistant Editor; Caroline Wood, Editorial Assistant

The Design Lab: Kathleen Petelinsek, Design and Art Production

Library of Congress Cataloging-in-Publication Data

Simon, Charnan.
 The sillies / written by Charnan Simon ; illustrated by Kathleen Petelinsek.
    p. cm. — (Magic door to learning)
 Summary: Illustrations and simple rhyming text show how silly two sisters can be.
 ISBN 1-59296-627-6 (library bound : alk. paper)
 [1. Play—Fiction. 2. Imagination—Fiction. 3. Sisters—Fiction. 4. Stories in rhyme.]
 I. Petelinsek, Kathleen, ill. II. Title. III. Series.
 PZ8.3.S5874Sil 2006
 [E]—dc22   2006001409

A book is a door, a magic door.
It can take you places
you have never been before.
Ready? Set?
Turn the page.
Open the door.
Now it is time to explore.

Lily was a silly.

4

Sam was silly, too.

Together they
were as silly
as the monkeys
at the zoo.

9

They were silly in the bathtub.

11

They were silly in their beds.

12

They often went
out walking wearing
lampshades on
their heads.

"Lily!" said her sister,
"Let's pretend that
I'm a dog!"

17

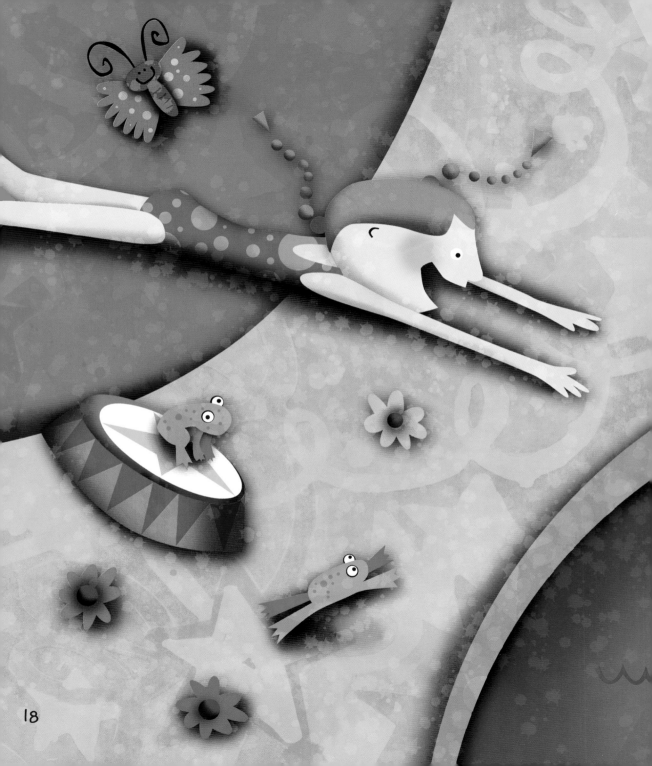

"Watch out!" shouted Lily,
"I'm a Sam-eating frog!"

Yes, Sam and
Lily were sillies,
as everybody knew.
Their parents
never scolded . . .

. . . because they
were silly, too!

Our story is over, but there is still much to explore beyond the magic door!

Do you like to dress up and pretend to be someone or something else? With an adult's help, create a mask so you can pretend to be your favorite animal—just like Lily and Sam did! Use crayons and markers to draw an animal's face on a paper plate. Have an adult help you punch holes on the right and left sides of the plate. Weave a string through the holes, and tie on your mask! Now you're ready to pretend!

These books will help you explore at the library and at home:
Katz, Alan, and David Catrow (illustrator). *I'm Still Here in the Bathtub: Brand New Silly Dilly Songs.* New York: Margaret K. McElderry Books, 2003.
Palatini, Margie, and Barry Moser (illustrator). *The Three Silly Billies.* New York: Simon & Schuster Books for Young Readers, 2005.

About the Author
Charnan Simon lives in Madison, Wisconsin, where she can usually be found sitting at her desk and writing books, unless she is sitting at her desk and looking out the window. Charnan has one husband, two daughters, and two very helpful cats.

About the Illustrator
Kathleen Petelinsek loves to draw and act silly. She lives in Minnesota with her husband, Dale; their two silly daughters, Leah and Anna; their two dogs, Bob and Rex; and one funny cat named Toed. (He has six toes.)